SUDDEN HARBOR

ALSO BY RICHARD FOERSTER

Transfigured Nights

Sudden Harbor

*For Marlene,
at Fundación Valparaíso,
these first efforts*

poems by

Richard Foerster

*Richard Foerster
X.26.97*

ORCHISES WASHINGTON 1992

Copyright © 1992 by Richard Foerster

Library of Congress Cataloging in Publication Data
Foerster, Richard, 1949-
Sudden harbor / Richard Foerster
p. cm.
ISBN 0-914061-28-3
I. Title
PS3556.O23S8   1992
811'.54--dc20   92-27943

ACKNOWLEDGMENTS

I am grateful to the editors of the publications in which these poems, some in earlier versions and with different titles, first appeared:

Abraxas: "Pilgrimage," "The Old Neighborhood" / Angelstone: "Eve" / The Anthology of New England Writers: "Maternal Grandmother," "Salz" / Antigonish Review: "A Mere Freak, They Said" / The Atavist: "A Sighting of Whales" / Boulevard: "108 1/2°" / Croton Review: "Dialogues of the Carmelites" / The Denny Poems: 1987-1988: "Bluefish" / Epoch: "Passings" / Green Mountains Review: "Boulders," "The Scream" / The Hollins Critic: "That Other" / Key West Review: "Again," "Shorebirds in October" / The Manhattan Review: "Isaac" / Nantucket Review: "Nantucket's Widows" / The Nation: "Halley's Comet," "Kreuzberg," "Ringing the Changes," "Windows at the Metropolitan" / Nebo: "Men's Group Therapy" / The New Criterion: "Sunset Sestina" / Onionhead: "Hairdo" / Pendragon: "Shore Stones in August on the Coast of Maine" / Piedmont Literary Review: "Orpheus' Return" / Poetry: "EEG," "Love Affair," "Playland," "Sleep," "Transfigured Nights" / Poetry Review: "The Hohntor" / Poets On: "The Superintendents of 3152 Hull Avenue" / Remington Review: "In a Formal Boxwood Garden" / Riverwind: "Sea-Changes" / Shenandoah: "King René's Book of Love, Folio 47v" / South Coast Poetry Journal: "At the Church of the Assumption" / Southern Humanities Review: "Fear of Earthquakes," "On the Train from Brighton" / Southwest Review: "The Day Stalin Died," "Ghosts" / Stone Country: "Medusas" / Tar River Poetry: "Crossing Over," "The First Harvest," "The Steel Ring" / Works in Progress: "Leaves" / Xanadu: "Sphinx"

Cover design and art by Gail E. Robinson
Copyright © 1992 by Gail E. Robinson

I wish to express my deep gratitude to the MacDowell Colony and the Virginia Center for the Creative Arts for providing me with the creative solitude in which many of these poems were written, and also to Robert Phillips for his constant encouragement and advice.

Manufactured in the United States of America
Published by Orchises Press
P. O. Box 20602
Alexandria
Virginia
22320-1602
G 6 E 4 C 2 A

for my friends

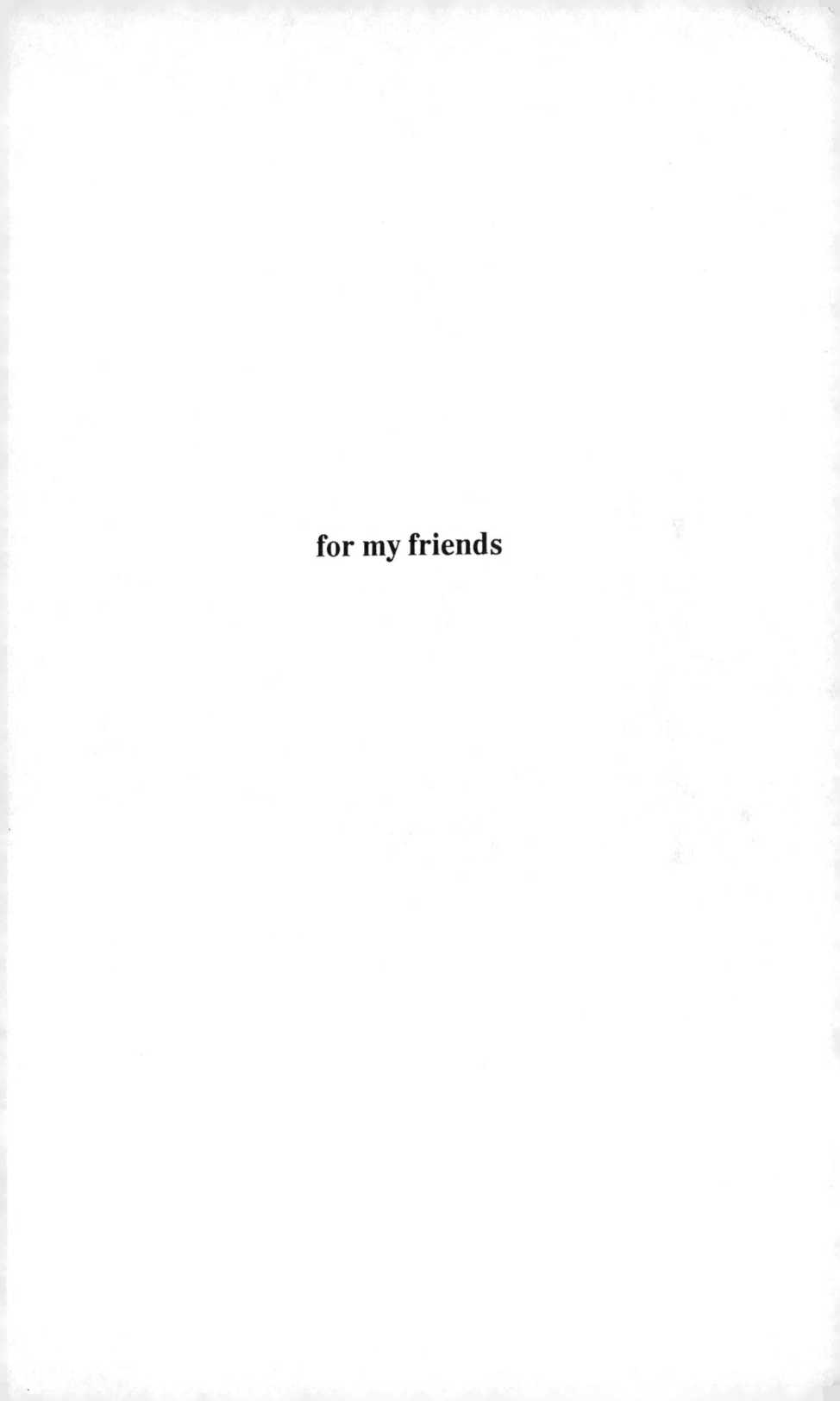

CONTENTS

ONE: THE PASSAGE

Salz / 13
The Superintendents of 3152 Hull Avenue / 15
The Day Stalin Died / 16
Crossing Over / 17
The First Harvest / 19
The Steel Ring / 20
Family Farm / 21
Maternal Grandmother / 22
Reeperbahn Sex Show / 23
A Mere Freak, They Said / 25
The Romantic Way / 26
Kreuzberg / 27

TWO: BRONX

The Old Neighborhood / 31
Bluefish / 32
Bathtime / 34
The Scream / 35
Passings / 37
Isaac / 40
Ghosts / 41
Christmas Eve / 42
Windows at the Metropolitan / 44
Bronx Park / 46
Playland / 47
108 1/2° / 49
Leaves / 51

THREE: THE BOXWOOD GARDEN

At the Church of the Assumption / 55
Pilgrimage / 57
Eve / 58
In a Formal Boxwood Garden / 59
Sphinx / 60
Dialogues of the Carmelites / 61
Shore Stones in August on the Coast of Maine / 62
Nantucket's Widows / 63
A Sighting of Whales / 64
Medusas / 65
On the Train from Brighton / 66
Men's Group Therapy / 67
The Hohntor / 68
Hairdo / 70
Orpheus' Return / 71
Ringing the Changes / 72
Again / 74

FOUR: PILGRIMAGE TO MOLENBEEK

Sunset Sestina / 77
EEG / 78
Principia / 80
That Other / 81
Sleep / 82
Halley's Comet / 83
Shorebirds in October / 85
Boulders / 86
The Swans / 88
Sea-Changes / 90
Transfigured Nights / 92
Love Affair / 94
King René's Book of Love, Folio 47v / 95

Sudden Harbor

ONE

THE PASSAGE

Salz

Like a vignette in the deep perspective
of a Flemish master, the town my father left
in 1928 seems far removed from foreground drama,
yet here in the shade of the linden tree,
a Holy Roman emperor sat, consolidating peace.
In its crown, my father claimed, white storks
nested throughout his boyhood. But now
the limbs — blasted by a thousand years,
braced and barely green — no longer cradle
soaring omens. The Virgin, too, is gone
from her azure niche atop the door
to the half-timbered house and stableyard
where my father tended raucous geese like a lord
with a willow switch. Today the windows,
once bright with geraniums, stare blankly down
at the narrow street, scrimmed with the cataracts
of years. But over all these ghostly emanations,
the lapis-blue spire of the church still rises above
the other four that crouch like small evangels
at its foot. There my father shivered through winters
in a rough-hewn pew worn smooth with a family's
devotion. At altarside a squat coal stove once blazed
for the parish priest like an ancient superstition.
Which Sunday was it he withheld the rigid wafer
from that foolish girl in finery, the aunt I never saw?
My father's knuckle-blow burst like a charge

from the shadows of the church-close wall. Across the years it stings, like salt on a festering wound.

The Superintendents of 3152 Hull Avenue

In that basement apartment of first memories
I looked out of a skeletal whale,
the ribbed cage of my bed, out through
a deep-silled window, into midday
caught as a brief slant of sunlight.
There in the narrow sunken yard she'd send
me out to play beside the rough
foundation stones, which even now,
just one of memory's ruins, seem colossal.
The only colors were the blue straight up
and the persistent sumacs' green that sprang
from any crevice in those walls and hung
in midair, exotic as tropic palms
to a Bronx boy. My father hacked off all
that he could reach, as if grayness were
a virtue he could never quite perfect.
Instead, it was my mother who completed
those walls, gave them their lasting texture,
granular and oily, as soot will be:
Wandering back inside from play,
I found her, in a cavern heaped with coal,
stooped before open iron doors, feeding shovel
by shovel her secret uncontainable god.

The Day Stalin Died

I heard the muffled baritone report
spill like fog about the polished deep
mahoganies of my mother's living room.
I must have been at play, at some four-year-old's
puzzle rivaling the intricate
design of the Oriental rug, as the old
Majestic, an electric grandmother's clock
with a Thirties radio in its womb, bore
its incongruities once more beneath
the placid face of time. Fireside chats
must have crackled through that gauzy grille,
then infamy and victory, big bands
and the bomb. A miracle, I thought,
that tubes as bright and empty as Christmas balls
could pluck a voice from air. But that grande époque
and tyrant passed like the flash of a parlor
trick: When the first irreplaceable cylinder of light
went dark, my mother had the anachronism
gutted and shelved for bric-a-brac.
In my parents' eightieth year, a German porcelain
goose girl and a smiling chimney sweep
were all they chose to salvage of the past.
Today I glanced into that mute and burnished face
and stared at the illusory stillness, the separate
path I take along the orbit of its slower hand.

Crossing Over

I was six, in the transatlantic
toss of a spring storm.
On the vast floor of the ballroom
emptied by seasickness, the cards
I dealt for solitaire
with each pitch and yaw of the ship skimmed
the veneer like catamarans
in some exotic cove.
The portholes were capped tight
with steel. The vessel groaned.

What seemed years passed before passengers
stalked the promenade.
As I peered at the immense gray
turmoil, at waves, gunmetal scud
lidding the horizon,
I shook with the cold electric pulse
of a cry, *Boat! Look. There. A boat!*
A yawl, masts storm-blasted,
slid along the swells, sank
into the troughs, and rose

a clinging dream, like slime-weed on stones
exposed at low tide.
Who strained at the wheel and witnessed
the wind's talons raking the sails?

Three decades past, I find
the flotsam of that time and begin
again a voyage — ignorant
still of the sailor's fate
one day from Newfoundland's
taut, familiar moorings.

The First Harvest

Salz an der Saale

I sat atop a tractor, still as bronze.
My cousins had propped me there
and turned to drawing windrows
into haycocks and ricks.
                      I saw
everything but me was bending
earthward. The hills were round
with a history they knew nothing of.
Above the town a hawk was falling
on a yard of chickens, its wings
arced for the plummet, even in death.
Somewhere a farmer, perhaps my uncle,
was lowering a gun, was counting
his wealth in feathers.
                    There in the field
which my cousins will someday divide,
their backs were ripening like stalks
of grain burdened with sunlight after rain.
A green dust from the hay was settling
over my clothes and skin. I was too old
to cry. If I don't move now, I thought,
I will be buried alive.

The Steel Ring

The bull was howling at first light,
straining his flanks like bellows.
The whole countryside fluoresced
with the sound when he caught
his steel ring on the bolt
of the pasture gate. He wouldn't let up,
but seethed back and magnified
his pain in proportion to weight
and will.
       Unnatural—such terror
in mighty eyes, the ring torn free
of the rubbery flesh, the beast
gone mad, and blood, blood
beneath the cauterizing glow
in my uncle's steady hand.

Family Farm

Years after, visiting my cousins' barn
where the cows are kept life-long
in filtered light, away
from the patchwork of winter
wheat and barley — my father,
who'd sold his birthright cheap
for passage to the grid-blocks
of the Bronx, complained of the flies
that sipped at the dark still pools
of the cattle's eyes and twitched
their ears like Hera's curse: *"My* father
never permitted such disgrace."
Nearby, silent, I wanted to escape
that shrine to inexhaustible patience
and the god's mutating love.

Maternal Grandmother

Hamburg, 1956

I wonder what she thought of that tow-head child
from America, all eyes in a foreign land, unsyllabled
in even the simplest German courtesies, and willful

as sin. She never spoke to me, or touched — a monument
apart, she sat in my uncle's kitchen in Altona, weighty
as a Hohenzollern queen. Bemedaled by the Reich

for bearing eighteen bodies to the Fatherland,
she was, when I beheld her at eighty,
no Valkyrie or Circe or wife. Now I wake

to dreams of northern seas where white immensities
approach, threatening and serene. I watch
from my bedroom window the fertile moon each month

burgeon from black depths beyond the vigilant
seamark's sweep and think at times how the last
survivor in a distant outpost of empire

must have felt recalling a face like hers.

Reeperbahn Sex Show

Hamburg, 1984

From a high-backed crescent booth, I stared,
half-eclipsed, into the halogen glare

where "Sammy and His Girls" were employed
in an up-dated sort of morality play

on the subject of German eugenics.
A palm-fronded set, less than authentic,

suggested a Kamerun outpost in days when big-busted
Fräuleins in khaki were victims of lust-

crazed chiefs—for so was "Sammy" decked
out, resplendent in leopard and one-foot erection.

The Fraus from the bus tour tittered and pointed
at "Sammy" in profile. The husbands, with impotent

smiles, nodded and sipped at their schnapps.
But when "Sammy" speared his three captives, hopped

from one to the next in rapid succession with guttural,
fluent, High German groans, a chorused gasp of *Mein Gott*'s

rose from those black-leather booths. After the bows

and applause, the clatter of glasses, houselights redoused

through a series of bodies — I stood in the congealed

neon light outside, by the church where my mother kneeled

seventy Augusts before at the start of war. There, the one

I'd seen was walking with his wife and son.

A Mere Freak, They Said

for Harriet

Descending the steps of the loggia
by the Theatinerkirche,
we surveyed the grandeur
and disgrace Munich is heir to:
everywhere the quiltwork
of centuries in the restored
facades; nowhere the seductive
harangue, except in the echoes
deep in the brain — That morning

the pavements glistened with hail
and shivered glass, a freak
of German weather. Citizens
marveled at the pockmarked
cars, the tattered awnings.
Nearby, a shopkeeper dutifully swept
the sharp light into dustpans
while glaziers were already busy
hoisting brilliant new banners skyward.

The Romantic Way

Rothenburg, Dinkelsbühl, Nördlingen — like boats
emerging from a mist, adrift with unreality,
Flying Dutchmen, neither in nor out of time —
where could they carry three exiles, moonstruck
as we were by their turrets, cobbles, and moats?

To graveyards with shattered stars of the long-ago
expelled. Through shrines to the Maiden's spiked embrace
and ancient churches with noseless Madonnas
reformed to Lutheran tastes. Then into the empty
cloister bakery where the Death once swelled like dough.

But what could truly touch us half a millennium
from their tortures and their plagues? The flowers
at every window blazoned like robed choirs extolling
that summer day, and in the Burggarten where we lingered,
lindens, busy with the commerce of the air, hummed

a melody of forgetfulness of all but then and there.

Kreuzberg

in the Rhön Mountains, Bavaria

That first time, climbing with my father
up to the Kreuzberg, I found
a raven on the forest path—
soft as black talc on my fingers
when I picked it up, a lifeless luster.
Its wings unfurled as if pride
rather than death could still
bear it into flight. Now I wonder
whether it was a child's first waking
or just my eight-year-old's savage faith
that seized my thoughts that day and made me
insist on carrying that dark thing
to the mountaintop and lay it where Franciscans
had made a Golgotha. A child dwarfed
by such realism can wish for miracles,
can cry when the dead stay dead. I knew nothing
then of other German golgothas when I went away
uncomforted. And so years later, standing there again
before those emblems of sacrifice, remorse,
and unrepentance so high above the Fulda Gap
where armies had grown old with patience,
I looked down over that borderland and saw
the sutures that bound the ruptures of the past
and strangely summoned up that fallen scavenger
and my prayer for a healing.

TWO

BRONX

The Old Neighborhood

Watching a dust devil catch
last fall's leaves and tatters
of a *Daily News* — the years spin off

and once again I am at arm's length
whirling above his face in the boozy air,
giddy with trembling and laughter.

The el sows sparks up Webster Avenue.
The neon of Louie's Bar & Grill buzzes,
has its nervous twitch. Mother

waits four flights up, the blue
veins in her hands wrung dry.
I am lighter than a word

he never spoke. Had he let me go
I would have circled the rooftops,
never come down.

Bluefish

He brought it home in burlap,
eased it out tail first,
the way a hunter would
unsheathe a favorite weapon.
When he held it high, a long
sinewy thing, like a boy's
amputated leg, I watched
the gills swing wide on weakened
hinges and reveal the violet
blossoms dead inside.
Its fins lay furled against
the sleek hull, and the open mouth,
that savage ornament at the prow,
seemed startled with remembrance.
He lowered it into the deep
sea-gray metal sink and poised
the tip of his rusted blade
at the anus, slid it deftly in,
then forward toward the parabola
at the lower jaw, around and up
until the head with its sheening agates
slapped against the bottom of the sink.
By now the wound he'd made
gaped like a thing I'd never seen,
and the air in the basement smelled
of endless tides, of birth

and death, and yet I watched
while the snakes coiled in my gut
as he washed the wonders out
and, all grin, thrust them toward me
dripping from his hand.
But when he took up the blade again
and moved it over the limp slab
that had been so mighty, as if it now
were a whetstone, the scales
flew and fired my arms and hair
with isinglass, with such pearled lights
that when he held out his triumph
splayed across his palms I knew
nothing was there that was not mine.

Bathtime

Mine was the only color — a boy's
pale skin tingeing a porcelain world,
a small space leached of everything
impure, a multiplicity of white:
the wall's squared hierarchies, the floor's
tight hexagonals, tiles I'd count
time and again as if counting were a prayer
the nuns had taught, *God, make me clean.*
Then I'd rub the bar hard over my limbs
and secret places until I must have seemed
an Eros sculpted from Carrara marble.

Once my father swayed in, found me
transformed like that. He laughed
so loud his sour breath blent
with the soapy air. After he slid
the curtain shut, I sank into the tub
and watched the lather lift then swirl
like bandages from around infected skin.
When familiar sounds spilled, I peeked about
the curtain's edge. One by one shadowy words
I'd heard swelled with light, burst into a boy's
private litany for that red and warty hooded thing
he held so delicately.

The Scream

I never saw it, except in books,
and even then in black and white,
like a dream whose images are
unshakable but not quite clear,

and yet that picture of a sound
can come back unexpectedly,
like an aftertremor rising through
the underpinnings of the heart,

so that I want to know, as Munch
must have, when it is we first press hands
to ears and feel the very air we breathe
crushed beneath a scream. — Perhaps it was

that morning she took me in hand, when I skipped
across the pavement's cracks and lines, up
the hill, farther than I'd ever been allowed
to go alone. She brought me to the steps below

the broad high doors, where I stood
and craned to read the straight-backed letters
chiseled overhead. I had not noticed
she let go my hand until I turned

and stared back down the hill, across
the newly charted distance I had come, and saw
the fading pattern of her summer dress
tremble just an instant, like a fully hoisted sail.

Passings

1954

At the animal farm

my mother paid

one quarter for one

bottleful of milk so her child

could feed a lamb. And years

after I'd remember the empty bottle

and the second eager creature

that snapped and sucked at the rubber nipple

and fed on vacuum

in the glass. As it pulled I felt

the draw toward dark eyes, felt the drain,

white and rich, the rhythmic

flow as through a woman's breast

and grew whole at the moment of being

starved.

1962

Nine o'clock, the nuns

at the Sunday children's mass

in their black and white

prowled the graded territories

and kept me praying through
fingertips soldered together,
their sparks flying past hierarchies.
Bring, Bring, Bring — they taught me
how the moon can sear.
And later, when the imposition of innocence
weighted my eyes as I filed from the rail,
I'd hear, *Swallow!*
Swallow without chewing —
and feel that piece of bread
softly razoring my tongue.

1821

> *After three months adrift in mid ocean,
> the survivors of the whaleship* Essex
> *drew lots. The cabin boy lost.*

We circle on the rim
of hope where the sea ends
and swells into furze-scratch,
where goldenrod bend and burgeon,
where the earth is ripe against
the sky.
      But here, heaved
and blistered, we stare at a blank
plate and assume the life of flies

chanced through open casements
after Sunday dinner.

On the eightieth day, when the harpooner
died and Captain wrapped his heart
in canvas and dropped it over
the side, I prayed his flesh
would not fill me with voices.

But what part of me has he become
that I am bloated with silence —
with the patience of a frog I saw once?

His stare wandered past wanting depths
of ponds or islands of waterlilies
while a ribboned snake, from out of shadow,
closed its maw in smooth jerks
over his horizoned eyes.

Isaac

I saw first the dirt under his nails,
then the weathered hand wielding the bright
blade. My breath was but another ghost
in the cold, skull-lustrous air. Nothing
came of it: A ram wandered by—
a sign, he said, from the Thundering One.

That this victim struggled, that its fleece
smoldered, choked my father's every prayer
were never written—nor that I descended
from the high place that day, shouldering
the patriarch, no heavier now
than the few sticks he'd have burned me on.

Ghosts

Each Easter something green sprang
up in him: he'd take his squeezebox Kodak
and me to the Bronx Botanical Gardens.
Positioned in the sun and swarm of petals
and bees, I was rare stone beneath the squint
of his appraiser's glass.
                        But sliding prints
from yellow sleeves, he'd toss them down
at me: in one I stood beyond a faded summer
curtain, wrapped in gauzy light; a black swath
obscured my face in others. *You must have moved.*
Defective film, he huffed. I murmured, *Ghosts,*
in jest, not knowing how soon his gaze would fix us both
in ghostlike stares, beyond approach or change.

Christmas Eve

The parti-colored boxes under lock
and key I'd plundered weeks before. A weasel
could not have drawn the pleasure from an egg
as expertly as I forbidden peeks
from gift-wrapped toys. I'd haunted the apartment
for days, kept home from school with chicken pox,
in quarantine from friends. I watched the season's
scurry four flights down, brooded like an owl
in an empty barn, yet harbored secret joy:
The Bronx still lay mouse-brown before me, roofs
still tarry black, the sky too blue for snow.

My mother clerked near Woodlawn, basketed
bright marzipan on cellophane — red crystal-
studded strawberries, asparagus
I'd never eat except like that, and rain-
bow globes of quince, of tangerines.... I pictured
her there behind those cased confections, tiers
of cherry-centered cookies, powdered slabs
of stollen, mincemeat pies, but slowly
the mystery of sadness filled the rooms,
like incense during Benediction. Thanks,
unworthy thanks. How to unblight the apple,

those violated gifts beyond the neat
array of Sunday hats and pocketbooks?

Grown men, I'd learned, and growing boys don't pray,
but prey on what they want. My father now
that work was done was drunk at Louie's Bar
& Grill. A fact of life: the more time passed
before I'd hear my father's key tap-tap
then tickle at the lock, the likelier
a bear would lumber in, growl, claw at me.
And was it not like this: a boy propped at
a window, waiting an arrival, watching

the sun extinguished by the sprawling world,
and seeing, once the sky was exhausted of magic,
a star that he could plot his future by.

Windows at the Metropolitan

After traveling the dark tunnels on a dime, at ten,
I wandered the flood-lit maze of Renaissance Masters

(deserted then, unfashionable) and felt the allure
of windows behind the azure cloaks and pale crooked necks

of the Madonnas who seemed more distant and alien
than anything the nuns had taught. But there, beside them,

no more than a few inches square, in brushstrokes
fine as hairs, the artists had put infinity,

and I peered, close as the guards would let me,
and felt myself, in my ignorance, fall through

into landscapes a child could almost imagine
beyond a city's walls: near plains, far crags

and castles only the eye could climb,
floating like islands quiet and exempt

from thorns and hammer-blows, which I should have known
even then must attend the innocent ones in the foreground.

Though now I see a jest in those teasing vignettes
with their tiny glimpses out of time, I cannot pity

that exhilarated boy who turned at closing and rode the D train back to his lonely station in the Bronx.

Bronx Park

I feared bacchantic rages in that house
and hair-trigger neighborhood boys outside
loaded with epithets. And so I'd walk the worn
blue slabs down Hull Avenue, quickly
past the Gay Dome Bar, and escape
into my imperfect Eden, where
nature strove to beat the odds
wagered from the outset against it.

Tamed and patinating, the river still
held wonders enough for an urban boy.
Carp, brindled gold on gray, mouthed
widening O's to mine, while all above
among the virgin stand of hemlocks
birds I never saw but there trilled
their intricacies about a world I was not heir to.
Labyrinths of flyways riddled my sky

for years, till one warm March after school
when I was twelve, I stretched out hidden
on that bank, pulling at forbidden smoke,
while on the other side a couple, drawn
to the burgeoning green, ground hips
against pale hips. I watched till they had gone,
then stood, taut with sudden appetite
for greater exile — and never went back.

Playland

The 8-track clicked through tunes as we two
cruised from heady Bronxville down to Rye
in my '66 eggshell blue
Volkswagen. Jesuit-schooled, I tried

to be all a Catholic girl would want:
left hand suavely at the wheel; right hand
on her knee; plus bon-vivant
banter and the Lonely Hearts Club Band.

We joined the paired and wholesome troops
beneath the razzled night
and shrieked through Cyclone loop-the-loops,
then braved the hokey House of Frights,

but when my student's budget failed
we walked the dark along the shore.
There the steady obbligato of the male
swelled above the fun park's roar.

We sat by rocks and listened to the Sound's
clouded water lap, then clamber
and withdraw. I cupped her breast, wound
a finger through her hair. My tongue remembered

silent speech, but soon she pushed
my lips away and pointed with surprise:
Everywhere were phosphorescent fish,
a thousand up-turned saintly eyes.

108 1/2 °

They could not hold me tight enough,
at seventeen, a Proteus among sea lions,
and so I swelled to yeasty dough.

Each minute I was something new, unique:
An ox-necked boy. A giant with apples
for balls. A carnival freak.

I grew into a Tree of Knowledge and read
the interns' awe of me in furrows
and asides. My limbs entangled stars

as I floated beyond their probing fingers,
weightless as a lama in ecstasy.
How the doctors worshipped me,

their bright benevolent sun.
Even after the blankets frosted over,
suspending me like a frail bubble

in ice, I changed: The room crumpled
in my crucible. I poured glowing ore
everywhere, smoldering and formless . . .

Normal at last, one said, as he whiplashed
a silver thread in the air and peeled away

the sheet to expose the virus' handiwork.

I gazed from the heights of my pillow,
like a general upon a hard-won field,
but when the doctor let me touch those parts

that had so recently guarded my father's
only gift to me, the past rose
from my body, like smoke from cinders,

hissing that I'd never change again, but stay
trapped in that inhuman form—the last
and only son of an only son of an only son.

Leaves

Even in this January storm
the leaves of that stunted oak
at the middle of the deserted cemetery,
weighted heavy with ice,
hang for dear life, absurdly superhuman.

Not even he, who left his homeland
for all the wrong reasons, could boast
the strength of one of those leaves,
who, in his golden 1930 America,
clung to a church steeple
after the scaffolding gave.

First he let the paintbrush fall,
and then himself, and then a brittle faith
when the pastor would not pay
to mend a back broken in two places.
With his pregnant wife, he belonged
to a different parish. But I

whose branches have been snapped back
by forty winters, whose roots
spread among forgotten bones,
must still hold on to him,
a brown and wintering leaf.

Alfons Foerster, 1906-1990

the # THREE

THE BOXWOOD GARDEN

At the Church of the Assumption

Salz an der Saale

      About her, minstrel angels of the High
      Baroque protrude, the pillars of the altar
      coil, a monstrance glares, and fatted putti ply
the air like legged balloons. The era's vision faltered,

and yet the blue Madonna soars toward deeper blue:
      Her earthly weight transforms before our eyes
      from something pure to purer still, imbued
with destiny and destination realized.

      Her face, a paradoxic aureole,
      unshawled and waxing in such raw release,
      beams like a jeweled reliquary hold-
ing uncorrupted flesh through all these centuries.

I knew that face, adrift beneath me on the floor
      as I rode my flesh to an ocean's rhythm —
      Bernini's raptured nun, my paramour —
My lust engorged on hers. Across the Channel, with him,

      she leaves me staggered at the miracle
      of loss: a spark ascending through the night
      so high that I mistake it for celestial
fire, for proof that what I love is gold despite

the cinders showering down. O Queen of Night, suspended
between your deathbed and the galaxies,
please tell me when it was my marriage ended
that I may shed this weight that keeps me on my knees.

Pilgrimage

I wanted the ground to tell us
what it knew about those wild orchids
that year after year pleasured
no one except those, by chance,
who happened on their patchwork shade and light
beneath the hemlocks. We marveled
as we fingered the tight purses of flesh
anchored in a rotting bed
where nothing else grew.

And so we'd go there just for them
and a short while to let the needles
cling in the creases of our bodies.
Where we lay the wind parted
dark skirts from about our nakedness.
The stream wore over our feet
as if they were stone. How I wanted
the earth to draw us toward it
and whisper the names of children.

Eve

She sprawled across the bed in the winter sun.
The trees outside wagged their bony limbs.
Their shadows played upon her back
and stole so little warmth from her skin
she noticed nothing:

                      not geraniums on the sill,
defiant and red against the withered stalks
of chrysanthemums she tended through the fall,
                      nor the fragile song
of her canary as it hopped peg to peg marking time
in its cage,
                      nor even me in the doorway
shedding darkness behind me like clothes.
When I bent to kiss the mole on the small of her back
she woke.

In a Formal Boxwood Garden

Eel-black clouds and a promise
of change in mid-afternoon
shrouded us under a dull buzz
of wisteria. Purposeless
outcroppings of the garden
ranged beyond the purposeful
mind of the gardener.
He lopped them off, tended
the trellis laths,
and pretended not to notice us.

Around her talk of love
a bird's hysterical song
hardened like a speckled shell
around indifferent cells.
A cricket's monotony
hung in the air with her whispers.
The fly in her hair
understood nothing of beauty.
And I, understanding even less of love,
waited beneath the overcasting grays of her eyes.

Sphinx

She wanted the river there always
flat and pragmatic as a tape measure
but bearing an occasional felucca
up and down, its sails a pterodactyl
in an empty sky —
                      and the desert too,
a precious wound the sun's gouge
would never let heal —
                      and infectious heat
to make bluebottles swarm in the skull.

Evenings the fellaheen who palmed
our trays with tepid gin eyed her white
chemise, hovered over its rise and fall
in idle chatter.
                Her smile was the hieroglyph
they thought they understood. In the night
I knew they dreamed
                      the river had whitened with snow.

Dialogues of the Carmelites

Like Poulenc's nuns, the waves crest
one by one, poised before the ritual
collapse, the thundering slide
into the momentary silence
of the Terror's guillotine.
There are no small deaths
in opera.
      Yet the lovers nearby
too are tumbling—through the neon
haze of bars, back to rooms
with mosquito screens.
              On rented beds
they join in pairs like halves
of scallop shells. For a while
the ocean carries them. Its music
sweeps a blackened stage. Sunlight
is the blade.

Shore Stones in August on the Coast of Maine

The water moved like fire ants across our feet.
The children had an hour before sun and moon
would shift an ocean over their moats and keeps
and hide the stones we rifled for souvenirs.

Not one resembled the mathematician's
serene balloon, the perfect
blanched abstraction we skeletonized
on paper as students,
                      nor even a planet
in miniature, gouged from its orbit
and left in that low-tide slosh and sand,
nor a gannet's egg, nor a speck
of dust grown monstrous.
                      Not one conformed
in grayness: haphazard quartz streaked some;
scars mottled each in their way. Even as we stood,
the tide was working time's abrasion on the one
we thought was Swedenborg's skull.

Among those thousand other vacationers, we watched
the distant shapes of children, the evaporative
dream we drifted in, and held each other's hand
so tight our knuckles whitened, then knew
not all imagination would ever keep us whole.

Nantucket's Widows

Always she began the same.
On the balcony. Caught
in the moon's ragged tear.
Her footsteps tamping down
the powdery darkness
that would not let her sleep.

Pace. Clockbeat. Pulse.
I filled the silences she left behind.

Somewhere beyond the balcony
she'd wander with Nantucket's widows.
Many nights I watched their ghosts
against the wall, their backs turned
to empty bedrooms, solid
in their precise rectangles. And yet

how they could ease themselves into the air
and race with dolphins at the prow.

A Sighting of Whales

That this night could be different:
the ribboned light which paves the ocean's
pathway to our feet, the too self-conscious
touch of bodies that never wholly blend
except like air and water in moonlight.

It is reflection of reflection
that we see, a bedazzlement
that hides the silent carnage underneath —
A dark shape like a disembodied hand
rises above the passive sea of smiles,

takes aim and fires blackness sundering white.

Medusas

The jellyfish still bob in some twilight tide,
star-backed and aimless,
each spreading its dome above
a universe that trails
into the darkness I did not enter
out of fear.

A well-tanned native girl rode the swells
and chided me with a voice that welled up
from the otherworld.
Her hand clamped down round the center
and tossed up a jellyfish near my feet.
I watched its ooze slip through

the sand and disappear.
This is the way it will be from now on —
Her face will swim and cast
deathmask smiles at me
through the black resurgence
each time I look up at the stars.

On the Train from Brighton

One evening slipping
through the vaulted light
of Victoria Station

we arrived at the end
of an afternoon in the sun
and waited

for the shudder and the gasp
before descending
to the platform,

but despite her arm
in mine I felt that this
was what it meant

to be a childless man
and wife: two lives
laid out like rails

stretching endlessly back
from that singular future
which they had misbegot.

Men's Group Therapy

Look at the men in the therapist's room:
Their callused fingers mass like eels
hauled writhing from their private gloom.

They talk of scoreless weekends, doomed
affairs, their wives' lost sex appeal.
Look at the men in the therapist's room

shift in their seats, details cocooned
for fear the truth might be revealed
and hauled writhing from its secret gloom.

Each yearns to let his passion bloom
like a cobra's hood and strike at the heel —
Look at these men. In the therapist's room

no one is impotent. Presume
no lust for boys remains concealed,
held writhing in its private gloom.

At session's end each one resumes
his stature, strides out masked in steel.
Look at the men from the therapist's room,
hauled writhing toward their private gloom.

The Hohntor

Bad Neustadt/Saale

For centuries the swallows have
erupted into evenings, down
from the High Tower's hollow eaves,
and soared above my father's town.

Scores twitter, flare the halflight, now
in wargame squadrons, now alone,
rapt in purposeless delight. How
will I face the dark when they are done?

I sit within the medieval
battlements and stare, no more secure
than those whom the swallows' revels
eased when the tower stood at war.

Beyond, all of my family lie
scattered in this valley's churchyards.
How should a final son reply
to a dour monument that guards

the ever changeless and the changed?
This congregation worships it
with flight ecstatically arranged
above me in the violet

nimbus of the sun's last rays.

Before night snares them, each bird ducks

beneath the tower's roof. Why praise

their roost, this constancy, this flux?

The absence surges — slackened

drive, the wayward wife, our weaseled love —

but then, around this blackened

edifice, the stars begin to move.

Hairdo

That night in our second-floor hotelroom
overlooking the commerce of the parking lot
where girls' bare legs in late October stepped
smoothly in and out of cars, I waited naked
in the bed as she prepared herself, sealed
the dress up in its plastic bag, misted herself
with a negligee and the now familiar scent,

and gazed, her back to me, into the silver pool
of her own regrets and expectations.
When finally she came to me, for foreplay
she asked that I remove the bobby pins
girdering the upsweep of her curls.
I counted . . . *forty-eight, forty-nine, fifty* . . .
as my fingers searched ever deeper

through the mysteries of another man's creation.
Slowly the marvel came undone:
a hundred pins, as if one more or less
would have missed perfection — and afterwards,
looking down at that unruly thing,
like a prop for the final act of a tragedy,
I hid my face in the chaos I had made.

Orpheus' Return

So this is the gift:
a dawn widening
like a wound through linen.

Last night her face moved close,
an urgent moth, spell-drawn
to my dream: I stretched out hands,

so sure in that otherworld,
and plucked — at nothing,
scorched and crippled wings.

And now this broad space,
passive and cold, pools
with the inescapable

agonies of the commonplace
and waits for the next and the next
miraculous ascent.

Ringing the Changes

Plain hunting, treble bob, grandsire—
One upon the next, the whole bronze choir

tumble through the permutations
with insidious logic, no theme

but change, and nothing to assuage
the on-rushed calligraphic stream

along the border of the page.
It's algebra's emotion, sums

of sound piled layer by layer
atop these stones and mumbled prayers.

The last tone lingers, fades like love
or memory of love reproved

by ravenous silence, the state
of dissolution to which all

works come. Where is the melody,
the revolutionary phrase scrawled

across the mind's altar, the debris
we pick through to reorchestrate

lost symphonies? The church is still.

I sit, poised like a bell, and peer

through the terrible gaping O

of the soul's circumference, toward fear,

or its reflection, far below.

Inside, a peal begins to spill:

Change. Change. Change. The pattern grows unique

as forged shapes swing skyward — and speak.

Again

Were I to close my eyes, I'd hold time,
hold you. So like the tallow moon
on ocean's rim before its climb
and diminution, bonds too soon
go slack. Its blanching stare impugns
the dark. I'd say it was sublime,
were I to close my eyes. I'd hold time,
hold you. So, like the tallow moon,

it's just lapsed memory that primes
these tides and makes my brain balloon
with youth's shadow pantomime —
and yet, why should I be immune?
Were I to close my eyes, I'd hold time,
hold you, so like the tallow moon.

FOUR

PILGRIMAGE TO MOLENBEEK

Sunset Sestina

Like symphonic melodies, they unhinge,
return remade. I'd have them delight
with sameness and change. When daily
the sun diminuendos, flames the coast
of Maine, eases, teases with certainties,
I'd believe any going blazons bright at coda.

Today the sun's tinge tickles the curls, singes
the breakers, shudders windows and delights
like cymbal-shimmer. The lobster boats that daily
heave green-hulled delve, then coast
glissando back to port. Their V'd certainties
wing aft, and gulls, like pink iotas,

imprint the impressionable sky with their daily
accusations. Now gluttonous shadows delight
at feasts, grow fat in corners, and the eye must coast
upward like a rising curtain. Tree-

tops, rooftops strain at alpenglow. The daily
drift slips like string through fingers. The delight-
ful balloon climbs on sighs of remorse, boasts

of wonder. How untiringly I crane after these daily
departures, nature's scheduled flights.

Night after night their dark notes assail me.

EEG

A Colorado skyline abstracted,
my scenery of thought scrapes along
the paper. To the white-smocked woman,
a head is merely an unstable planet,
as lacking in mystery as the Richter scale.
She waits beyond the glass in her fragile glow
for the ineluctable electric lapse
fluttering on the graph —

                         In Bruegel's world
contorted trees mimed the annual parade:
the epileptics' pilgrimage to Molenbeek.
As bagpipes whined, the accursed were charged
to dance on a bridge and coax their daemons
to trembling. And so faith's tarantella forced
the poisons out into the turbulent stream.
On the far bank the devotees sat, emptied
buckets on the grass —

                         Lying here, my scalp
thumb-tacked and wired, I recall a high street
near London, double-deckers grinding past,
the restless queue, the sudden carillon
and sidewalk's embrace, and, later, furtive stares
and speculation (drugs or drink?). A squirrel-gray
man asked if I wanted to come round for tea.

I answered distantly. From underwater.

An ondine. Apart.

               Time and place drift here
like medusas in the happenstance of ocean.

Their pearlescent tentacles trawl the dark

unconscious, sting and snare, then haul up

toward the light the unbelieving, depthless eyes.

As I sat aboard the bus that afternoon,

the gray Thames flared with colors when we crossed.

So now, for her, may they pour out on the graph

and limn this fluid world.

Principia

In the dream a tiny boat floats
beneath the unscalable face

of a glacier, pale as moonstone,
accretion of a continent, a history

moving grudgingly to the sea. Always
in this dream, fissures crack the mass

and the one watching from the boat can feel
the violent rending of a part from the whole,

the free fall and the splash because he is
no longer the man he was before

his eyes opened to this world.
He has become the dream, the body

plunging toward the sea, the after-
math swelling to a wave that arcs

outward, ever outward, past the fragile boat,
to disturb the starlit blackness just beyond.

That Other

In deep dark it stirred
its arms like moonlit wind
through unleaved trees in autumn.

I felt it rise from beneath
the earth and heard it cry
against the windowpanes.

When I awoke, the birches
moved like metronomes
and I shouted at this terror

seizing me, pulling me
back to its lips. Its phallus
burned like a brand against me

and mine against it. I saw
in those eyes my eyes. Its passion
tasted like mine. It grew

to flood the whole room as I sank
away beneath it. From a great
distance I saw this raw beast,

naked and still lustful, stalk
from my bed, then knew it was real—
like a poem that I had made.

Sleep

for Dana Gioia

When finally the headland slips away,
the voices at the dock trail after you,
arcing across the water like streamers
vibrant with wishes for your quick return.
But even as you strain to grasp the last
uncoiling strand, it sinks into the dark.

You might think you set out on this voyage
unprepared for the faces that well up
with gauzy luminescence from the deep
or glide across a ballroom or your bed.
The shudders, smiles, the enigmatic twinge
of shame are baggage you've unpacked before.

Only dimly can you know each stateroom
is your own, or that the sudden harbor,
bewilderingly clear and clangoring
with commerce and the stevedores' foul shouts,
is but the merest prelude to the vast
land you must call home.

Halley's Comet

I envied the muscled arms of the older boys
who controlled the deafening buzz and spin
of the gas-powered model planes that whirled

each Saturday above a Bronx Park field
up and down, restrained by two thin wires
predictably through orbits around those boys'

firm grips and concentrating stares. Weak-limbed
and amazed, I doubted I'd ever wake
like them to a universe where I stood like the sun.

Afternoons, corralled in the children's section
of the Mosholu Branch, I thumbed picture-
book astronomies and took in every page

as fact: Jupiter's miscounted moons, Saturn's unique
artglass rings, domed bases by the nineties
in cool Venusian valleys. And yet I kept faith

with one: that ominous Bayeux rocket stitched
above King Harold's crown, that certain
wonder, whose sky-length tresses in a photo from 1910

I never forgot. Even crouching like a hamster
once a week in Saint Brendan's School,
assured by nuns that desks could protect

against imploding glass, that a coat
furring me from head to toe could shield
my skin from radiation, that prayers mouthed

in stifling air would save me
for this world as surely as my miraculous
medal would save me for the next, even then I

never doubted the covenant we had.
Such scarred dreams have brought me
to this starred night, here where pines

and birches ring a meadow's open eye.
Tonight I know the world is straining
in darkness, puzzling at this predicted light.

I hold it in the glasses' circle, a wanderer
among the ancient gods and heroes — a fizzling squib,
slowly abrading in the black, like a meager promise

vengefully kept. When I lower my arms
and turn to walk back by flashlight, I am amazed
at how easy it was to let it go.

Shorebirds in October

The waves retreat, leaving a steam-rolled stretch
down Long Sands Beach, where a sea-soaked Irish setter
is chasing a flock of sandpipers. The dog thinks *Go fetch*
and gallops the thin sheen, getting wetter and wetter.

Like a brassy god, nymph-struck, he reaches his prize
as they veer off then bank, in Blue Angel formation,
back and forth. Though escape would be easy, they tantalize
the ungainly, indefatigable dog.

What made these lithe Ariels pause in their long migration
to play, just days ahead of the rattling cogs
of the season bearing down the coast like a tank?

Someone whistles, and the dog trots off, realizing
the familiar urgencies of home, giving thanks
perhaps for a glimpsed grace, this brief visitation.

Boulders

They nestle in the brown sponge
of the glacier bed like the abandoned

eggs of some hulking thing
this earth has long forgotten.

Crewelwork of lichen, blue-
green bruises, blooms about them.

Hydra-rooted balsam firs
cleave a few to their cores.

We spread a red-check cloth across
the broadest back and sit astride:

stately maharajahs, smug
anachronisms, picnicking.

Suddenly they rise and lumber back
the long road far to the North

away from this whittled landscape
back through secret passes under

pinnacles as gray as they, then
disappear into preutterance,

into that icy, grinding din before

Pleistocene and *Jagannath* and *Hasdrubal*.

The Swans

Glimpsing them by chance from the roadside
through a narrow windway in the trees,

we watch them glide the calm lake with magic
ease, then tip their behinds up obscenely

to browse the muddy bottom of its greens.
They are everything and nothing like

the incarnate spirits of water and air
our ballooning hearts burst for as children

when we read of the girl who knitted briers
into cloaks for seven swans, unbewitching them

with her bloodied fingers back into brothers.
Emblems of solitude and long retreat,

they do not seem to care their wooing cries
break through the leaves with all the pain of poets

as we listen and watch them now with none
of the innocence, sincerity, or grace,

none of the martyrs' zeal and faith
that propelled us through the maze of childhood.

And so, returning to the car, we almost snigger

at the thought that here in the questioning

curves of their necks and rigid, proud displays

of whitest plumes or in the brutal bill

and the cob's furious tread is the mythic

magnitude of desire and universal self.

Sea-Changes

for D. R.

1

A patient strapped to a bed, gray delirium
seething his limbs: the tide coils in waves, then sinks,
exhausted into a purled mirror. Gale winds thrum,
yet sandpipers tip-tip their backs to the blue-inked
expanse, feed at the edge of extinction, glide, land,
skitter onward, scavenging the warring strand.

2

Thin fog slithered in. Tonight's a black pearl.
Couples prowl its rare luster, drift muted
in moonlight among the dunes. Their arms curl;
their voices twist and spread like vines rooted
in darkness. Wide-eyed, the sea stalks the beach,
and I wonder what depth I cannot reach.

3

Ogunquit, Moody, Wells. Pale tracings
of frail lights span the monochrome

sea and sky. How my lost wife's face
flares like the moon's magnesium,
illuminates all here and now—
until your touch. Skulled moon, go down.

4

From the absent millionaire's cliffside deck
we watched the Atlantic whipped into mounds
of suds and a seagull's aeronautic
grace as it faced the Sirens' wail, swung round,
and deftly lighted in our sheltered cove.
Is this lust's promise, the calm eye that's love?

5

A cormorant diving is emblem for the mind.
The bright fish it craves, more often than not, escapes
into that treacherous element by winding
so deep the bird's lungs give out. Futile pursuit saps
desire. By your side that day, the sea smooth, sunlit,
I'd no need to see that spark. I had become it.

Transfigured Nights

Each June they summon long-dead dusks
of childhood, times I scrambled with my jar

and swiped the air with cupped palms
for the pulsing gold-green prizes — these

fragile, harmless things. Their pooled glow
once filled my bedroom like a flare

toward which I navigated dreams.
But then the marvels gasped and flickered out.

This June so few puncture the languorous dusk,
unlike that newlywed year I saw thousands

churn like the tunnel of a wave and whorl
around me in a rapture I could scarcely share,

a raw flux of sex. They spawned a galaxy
of light above the graveyard where I'd gone

to lose myself among the weed-choked rows.
Soon I was reeling with my arms flung high —

a foolish man in the apotheosis of his childhood,
saying *O God. O God, never let this end.*

Of course, it did. And yet in each random spark
tonight I snatch back something of that boy's lost fire.

Love Affair

Driving west
on a back road,
top down, and the wind
tousling the gray,
I let the radio
thunder Siegfried's death
and funeral music.
Suddenly I am aware
my emotions are all wrong.
The autumn colors
crackle overhead,
and in the open blue
some geese in haggard V's
are forging south,
but though this is Maine
and the world is slipping
into dark and cold,
just for now I am
revving into orange flame,
a hero's afterglow.

King René's Book of Love, Folio 47v

for Sophie Wilkins

Striding between Generosity and Desire,
the Heart seeks shelter for the night —
Not allegory, but the sunset leafed with gold
fires the imagination to linger
with these travelers between a forest
no broader than a parasol
and a chapel wedged into the scene
almost as an afterthought.
A few clouds, suggesting Oriental kites,
prowl the brilliant air.
A roan horse in the foreground ripples into foam
while its companion's ample splash
flares from the grass into a white
chrysanthemum. The plume on one horseman's
cap streams up pale as a comet
against the hipped and supple silhouette
of hills. In this twilight, without allegory,
everything verges on becoming
what it must: the sun's disk tipped
with the rarest pigments sinks inevitably
into a cinder of itself, the clouds
bluster lamely and collapse
like a belief in dragons, and the horses'
miracles are exposed as lanky hair and piss —

But assuming the heart does seek shelter
when the day blazes its last revelation
and the forest brims with fear,
then this tranquil moment tenses
as we enter the place of our desire,
and the generous centuries come flooding home.